HYPE BRANDS

OFF-WHITE

KENNY ABDO

Fly!
An Imprint of Abdo Zoom
abdobooks.com

abdobooks.com

Published by Abdo Zoom, a division of ABDO, P.O. Box 398166, Minneapolis, Minnesota 55439. Copyright © 2023 by Abdo Consulting Group, Inc. International copyrights reserved in all countries. No part of this book may be reproduced in any form without written permission from the publisher. Fly!™ is a trademark and logo of Abdo Zoom.

Printed in the United States of America, North Mankato, Minnesota.
052022
092022

THIS BOOK CONTAINS RECYCLED MATERIALS

Photo Credits: Alamy, Getty Images, Shutterstock, ©jpellgen p.18/ CC BY-NC-ND 2.0
Production Contributors: Kenny Abdo, Jennie Forsberg, Grace Hansen
Design Contributors: Candice Keimig, Neil Klinepier, Laura Graphenteen

Library of Congress Control Number: 2021950290

Publisher's Cataloging-in-Publication Data

Names: Abdo, Kenny, author.
Title: Off-White / by Kenny Abdo.
Description: Minneapolis, Minnesota : Abdo Zoom, 2023 | Series: Hype brands | Includes online resources and index.
Identifiers: ISBN 9781098228552 (lib. bdg.) | ISBN 9781644947982 (pbk.) | ISBN 9781098229399 (ebook) | ISBN 9781098229818 (Read-to-Me ebook)
Subjects: LCSH: Clothing and dress--Juvenile literature. | Brand name products--Juvenile literature. | Fashion--Social aspects--Juvenile literature. | Abloh, Virgil, 1980-2021--Juvenile literature. | Popular culture--Juvenile literature.
Classification: DDC 338.7--dc23

TABLE OF CONTENTS

Off-White 4

Hype 8

All The Rage 14

Glossary 22

Online Resources 23

Index 24

Taking **streetwear** and fusing it with high-fashion, Off-White is a brand all its own.

Starting as an **intern**, Virgil Abloh used his brilliance and style to change the industry and become the biggest name in fashion.

HYPE

Abloh **interned** at Fendi in Rome alongside Kanye West in 2009. The next year, he became the creative director of West's company, Donda.

Abloh launched his **streetwear** brand, Pyrex Vision, in 2012. Fans immediately felt the hype.

By the next year, Abloh had rebranded his menswear label Pyrex Vision into Off-White.

ALL THE RAGE

In 2014, Off-White **dropped** a womenswear line. The collections were shown at Paris Fashion Week and received high praises!

Off-White's first **concept store** launched in Tokyo in 2016. The opening was so successful, two more stores opened in Singapore and Thailand shortly after.

Nike and Off-White **collaborated** on a sneaker line in 2017. It was called "The Ten." It took 10 of the most iconic Nike shoes and **reimagined** them. The shoes sold out immediately.

In 2018, the brand **collaborated** with IKEA to create furniture with a hyped-up twist for a new generation.

In 2019, the company **collaborated** with the Museum of Contemporary Art. Together, they released a pair of Nike Air Force 1's that became an instant must-have.

Abloh passed away at the end of 2021. He was only 41 years old. The demand for his Off-White work skyrocketed. People have paid up to $10,000 for shoes that were once only $190.

Even though Abloh left the world far too soon, the hype he and Off-White built around the fashion industry will last a lifetime.

GLOSSARY

collaborate – to work with another person or group in order to do something or reach a goal.

concept store – a shop that sells a carefully chosen selection of products that connect to a central theme.

drop – when something that is highly anticipated is released to the public.

intern – a student or graduate gaining experience in a professional field.

reimagine – to take an existing product or idea and turn it into something new. To rethink it.

streetwear – fashionable, yet casual clothing worn by followers of popular culture. It is heavily influenced by hip-hop and surf culture.

ONLINE RESOURCES

To learn more about Off-White, please visit **abdobooklinks.com** or scan this QR code. These links are routinely monitored and updated to provide the most current information available.

INDEX

Abloh, Virgil 6, 9, 10, 12, 20, 21

Asia 15

Donda (company) 9

Fendi (brand) 9

IKEA (brand) 17

Museum of Contemporary Art 18

Nike (brand) 16, 18

Paris Fashion Week 14

Pyrex Vision (brand) 10, 12

stores 15

West, Kanye 9